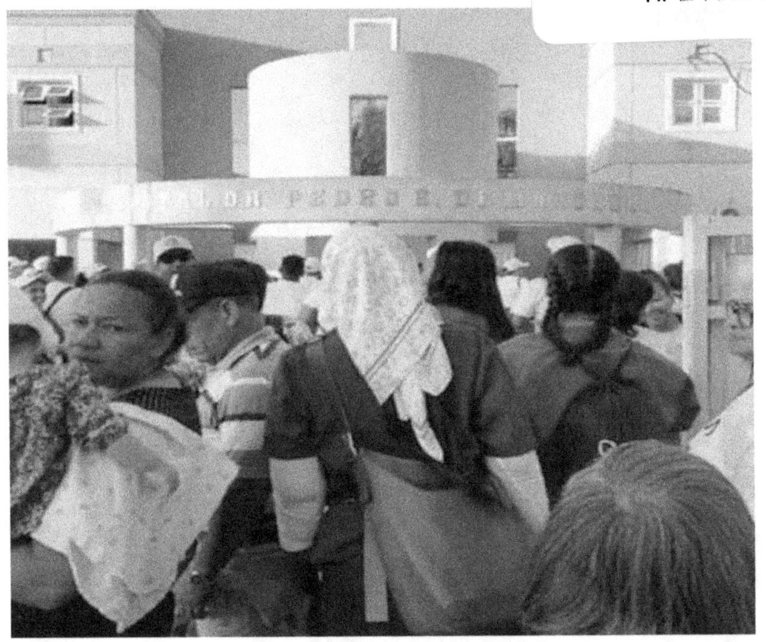

Holy Ghost on Fire:
A Missionary Work

Missionary Julian Marie Walker

Contributing Editor: All services completed by Imprint Productions, Inc.

Cover Design: All services completed by Imprint Productions, Inc.

Printed in the United States of America Published by Imprint Productions, Inc.

First Edition 2024

Many Are Called, Few Are Obedient

Original By: Ms. Julian M.Walker

Table of Contents

Table of Contents

"For the glory of God and the sake of the nations, we need to send more missionaries of color to the world"

-   *Unknown Missionary*

Introduction

Truth is not everything a man or woman says about you is the truth, but what God says about you. In the Bible God confirms this and affirms this in **Jeremiah 29:11 "For I know the thoughts that I think towards you, says the Lord, thoughts of peace and not evil, to give you a future and a hope."** This verse is a blessed covenant that most people take for granted. Webster defines the word covenant as an "agreement," but it is a promise from God our Creator.

Therefore, let's walk on faith and declare that our relationship with God is like binding a law contract from our birth to the end of life. If you have time just once read the first Book of Genesis in Chapter 1: 1-30 God spoke his words into the World.

God accomplished all that He spoke and in verse 31, He saw all that He made and declared that it was good. **Gen 1:31 "God saw all that he had made, and *it was* very good. And there was evening and the morning were the sixth day."**

Most of us only speak of the second covenant in Hebrew. So, I am not telling an old folk story, but how many of us are willing to admit that we are here on earth as spiritual beings living human beings' experiences? If it was not for our great ancestor's prayers, faith, bravery and covenant that God had with them, we would not have made it this far.

John 4:24 "God is Spirit, and his Worshipers should worship in Spirit and in truth." You can drop the mic now because God is even answering your ancestor's prayers from the grave.

Chapter 1

I know God says I am...

I believe that most time if we as God's people silence that voice of God in our hearts, that we would fall short of his true nature and calling for our lives. Thus, I am not judging anyone because that is above my pay grade but, it is clearly written in **Samuel 3:4 "The Lord calls Samuel, Samuel answered 'Lord here I am.'"**

I cannot tell you the countless times when I was silent my thoughts to hear my Father God's instructions and had not followed through with the instruction, especially in my younger years or because I did not want to offend another person or a family member.

Let me break it down so we are all on the same page. Do you know how you have a bad feeling about someone, or maybe you feel the vibe is off? Follow your gut instinct that is it right there! I am also not speaking of jealousy, lack of confidence, mental illness or other illnesses. I was not raised to disrespect anyone, if the truth be told I would get what you call a whooping, lashing or a spanking – which back then was a stricter form of love and discipline.

If I ever dare disrespect anyone – no matter what your name, age, nationality, or title – it would be corrected immediately. Respect was taught and given to everyone: "Yes sir," "No ma'am," "Good morning," "Good night," "Excuse me," "Thank you," "Goodbye," and so forth. I am grateful I am now empowered with the concept of faith and understand the power of prayer forgiveness and obedience.

Chapter 2

I Know Who I AM....

Today, here I go again, but this time with divine guidance. As iconic rapper Jay Z said in his song "Please allow me to introduce myself" because the woman you may have met three, two or one decade ago evolved and changed. This is a good thing because I am alive! I am first and foremost a daughter of the Living God, I was baptized in the name of the Father God, His Son Jesus Christ, and the Holy Spirit, I am Saved by God's grace, and nothing I could ever do on earth can wipe away God's gift of Salvation to me.

Yes indeed, to make this powerful introduction I am saying I live and conduct all my affairs through prayer, faith, and the acknowledgement of God's divine presence.

If you are saying WHAT? Keep reading.

Romans 10:9-10 The New International Version (NIV) says: **" 9 If you declare with your mouth, 'Jesus is Lord,' and believe in your heart that God raised him from the dead, you will be saved. 10 For it is with your heart that you believe and are justified, and it is with your mouth that you profess your faith and are saved."**

A Prayer of Salvation reads like this:

"Father in Jesus' name thank you for another opportunity to come before your presence I ask you now to forgive me for anything that I have done or said that has brought shame to your Holy name. I confess with my mouth, and I believe in my heart that God has raised Jesus from the dead and He now lives in me. I thank you, Lord, that I am saved, and I will serve you for the rest of my life, Amen."

I was giving this prayer to share with the world by a devoted missionary when I joined the Global Mission Team. Naturally, because I believe so strongly in this prayer that with my brother's permission, I had it printed in my mother's going Home Service program in June 2021 when she passed away.

It is so ironic that yesterday was her birthday and I

cried. I still have the birthday card and socks we bought for her. My brother, and I spent the day picking out flowers to give to her, only to discover when we got to the nursing home, that she was in very bad condition. No one called us or sent her to the hospital. However, when my brother and I arrived, they called for an emergency ambulance to take her to the hospital.

I was in New York for forty-five days visiting her because of declining health. One blessing was that my brother was by my side every day. When I finally flew from New York back to Georgia on January 6. I truly expected her to hold on and recover.

My mother taught us that we do not need many things to have a happy life when we have true love and the essentials. She taught us to always be respectful and never go to bed angry with anyone especially if you are married.

She was a kind woman who would give you her last dollar. She also taught us one of the most important principles of the Bible: to pay our tithes. We learned about tithing from the days when money was called "chapina" and "shilling."

She did not believe in shacking up; she believed in

marriage. She said that living together without marriage can make people forget why marriage is important. She taught me in a marriage your husband is the head of the family, and the home should always be respected. He should be your pastor, preacher, provider, friend, and lover. My mother was wise. She shared many other lessons too, but those were reserved for the worthy man.

She was a businesswoman, and she genuinely loved God. If she had one fault, it was loving her children and grandchild too much. She also said our dad was her greatest love.

To be honest, hearing that gave me the confidence to rise and become the best version of myself. Unapologetically, I know that I feel love, I am love, and I need no validation from anyone. Then I back it up with the scripture that says I am "fearfully and wonderfully made." That is my royal power.

And for the record, my dad said that she was his greatest love too. He once told me he and my mother took a bus to Clarendon to ask my grandfather for her hand in marriage. I thought that was beautiful.

You may be thinking I am getting off course, but as I

sit here writing, I am truly inspired by the song on my playlist by Wiz Khalifa: See You Again – "How can we not have to talk about family when family is all we got?"

When I say family, I didn't limit this to the bloodline. Thanks to all the kind people who were there for me and my brother. If the truth be told, they didn't have to stand with us, but they did.

Here's to all of you New Yorker and Georgia friends, the doctors, nurses and medical staff who provided care by telephone and video when I could not come home for my medical appointments – much respect and gratitude to you all.

Thanks to my daughter, Camay, for making sure I got home safely from New York to Georgia after losing my mom. Mommy loves you more than coffee.

At this point, the only thing left to say is that we honor her even through her sudden passing. I just hope she knows she was beautiful.

I am trying to move forward because I know that

she would want us to continue experiencing life and happiness – for her children grandchildren and great-grands.

If I had to sum up who she was, I would say she was kind, gentle, and loving. My mother, the Queen, was official and she will always be loved for many generations to come.

The grieving stage is still a process when it is a parent or husband. My mom would call me sometimes in the morning, if I did not pick up the telephone, she would always leave a message saying, "A mama, love you and call me later". Even the morning before she got sick, she called me and we talked, prayed, and laughed. Sometimes she told me what to send via UPS like clothes, and so forth. She never let me forget her dreams by saying to me, "Your brother was here this morning." It was her way of saying move back to New York. God's grace is priceless.

Chapter 3

Obedience

I had no intention of authoring this book, but you know the saying: "Obedience is better than sacrifice." I do not know who said it first; I just remember my mission director saying it whenever the task before us demanded so much. There were days when doing God's work abroad could have cost us everything.

One day in 2018, while on a mission trip to Belize, the group I was with was on its way to the airport to return home. However, our van stalled in a traffic circle. I was one of the twelve people awake in the van when I saw another pickup truck carrying a refrigerator almost crash into us.

The missionary men in the pickup truck behind us saw it too. All I could say was, "Father, not today," and suddenly the van engine started again, which saved our lives. We never really talked about it as a team afterward. We just understood.

Despite the trauma—which is often what happens when you go into the mission field—I cannot speak for everyone, but it definitely affected me. Mama Patrick once told me,

"When you become a missionary, your life will never be the same again," and she was right.

Being a missionary is not something you can put on and take off like makeup. You truly have to care about what God cares about and love what God loves. For me, pretending would never work because I only have one face, and I do not even know how to wear makeup. I stay true to myself and to the mandate God placed on my life.

Last week, I finally had the courage to ask one of my mission brothers if he remembered that day. He honestly said yes and reminded me of who we are, and that faith is our foundation.

You may be wondering what I am trying to say. Well, this is deep, calling unto deep, and only those who are truly called will fully understand.

As Dr. Martin Luther King Jr. said, "Faith is a living and unshakable confidence, a belief in God so assured that a man would die a thousand deaths for its sake."

First, I must say that I had no intention of attending the church where I have now been a member since January 1,2016. However, that Sunday morning, as I pulled out of my subdivision, The Vineyards, there was traffic, and somehow my truck simply followed the other cars right into the church parking lot.

I parked the truck and went inside the Church. I was astonished. Yes, I know the dictionary may not use this word for this moment, but to hear the singing and praising, I had never experienced anything like this before. It was as if I was at a live concert. It was like going to the old revival.

That Sunday morning, I saw a woman preaching.

She rocked my spiritual world. I had the opportunity to speak with her later and she said she was from a small island, and she was planning to move to Florida to be with her husband who was already there working. Please do not judge but I was raised in the old-fashioned Bible way. Men [man] are the preachers and Pastors. The woman was the pastor's wife, who ran Sunday school classes and was a marriage counselor for women and sometimes a teacher.

The "First Lady" was married to the Prime Minister, or the President who lived in the white house. I am not making this up. I asked my husband why women were not preachers or pastors, he smiled, looked at me, and said for the same reasons you cannot cook for three days a month. I still did not get it, so I asked him again why, and he said, "I can't give birth and have a baby." He could see I was getting upset because I did not like his answers, so he said it was uncleaned. I was upset at the end of the conversation and never brought it up again.

Here is the deal: I was young at that time, but I knew God came first and would continue to serve him. God was calling me, for his purpose and I did not know how to explain it to my spouse.

One Sunday morning during church announcements, they shared that they needed members to join the Global Mission Team. I did not think much about it because I could not afford the training, and I was already busy working on my Master of Business Administration degree. At the time, I was driving once a week to Ohio Christian University at the Morrow location for classes.

Later that week, I received a text message from the church saying that my pastor had decided to pay for the mission class and that I should call the director. I was honestly surprised because I had never seen another organization invest in its members that way.

I made the call out of obedience because, like I said before, graduate school requires focus, and I already had student loans on the line. The phone rang, and a sweet, high-energy woman answered. I explained why I was calling, and she simply said, "Yes! No problem. See you Saturday."

Honestly, I was shocked! Not only did she say yes, but she was also a lady with a boy's name—just like me. When I tell most people my name, I usually get shocked looks. I have been in classes where professors called attendance, and I waved my hand to let them know I was present and accounted for. But it was not until I said, "I am Julian, I am here," that they realized I was female.

It has been that way since grade school.

Yes, I am a girl, and I love it. It is fun seeing men's reactions. And if you are thinking, "WHAT?" Let me remind you—I am a saved woman, not dead.

Quick story.

When I was eighteen years old, I worked at the New York County Lawyers Association Library in Manhattan. One day, I was coming back from lunch and stepped onto the elevator. A handsome man looked at me and said, "Julian is a lucky guy."

I replied, "Pardon?"

He said, "You're beautiful, and your boyfriend is very lucky to have a girl like you."

For one quick New York minute, I blushed and answered, "I am Julian. This is my chain, and that is my name."

We both laughed and he said I'm calling you Billie Jean.

Maybe it was his deep California accent or maybe it was because he had seen me around while doing his legal research at the library, but that became his nickname for me until the day I met his mother in Queens, New York.

Through the years we remained good friends until he eventually moved to Africa. And yes, when I saw him again and he was married at the time. So, no – to whatever thoughts may be running through your mind.

Now, back to my calling and obedience.

I showed up that Saturday morning and introduced myself. Honestly, I remember thinking that her voice on the phone did not do her justice. She was even kinder in person. She greeted everyone warmly, and made people feel special.

That kind of gift only comes from God. Not everyone can do that. Not to overstate the truth, but it immediately put me at ease.

If the truth be told, I graduated from the Metropolitan College of New York with a Bachelor of Professional Studies in Human Services and Counseling. I left that university with the skills to become a good service provider to others and with the understanding that to truly serve God's people, you must love both God and His people.

That Saturday morning, March 4, 2017, the first official mission class met the rest of the new mission team members, including Mama and Papa Patrick, real missionaries who had lived and worked in Africa for many years.

They shared how they had a true heart for missions and had raised their children in Africa.

That day, I also met an iconic doctor whose name now appears on my certification for a short-term biblical mission abroad. She was amazing – there is simply no other way to describe her.

She has traveled to 150 Countries at times preaching, teaching, and helping countless families through sustainable outreach and support.

Her greatest gifts to the world were, and still are, providing clean water, building wells, supplying food, clothing, shelter, churches, schools, and medications. If people needed help, she did her best to provide it. Even today, she continues serving communities abroad by helping provide tiny homes.

She once said that women are risk-takers and she truly lives up to every word.

Here I go again, speaking my truth: this doctor on the mission field reminded me of Barbara Walters co-hosting on world news – bold, intelligent, compassionate, and unforgettable.

She inspired me to fully embrace the responsibility and desire to serve under the mandate of being a missionary.

For those reading this who may not fully understand what I mean, that was the day "Missionary Julian" was born.

I discovered a new passion for serving God's people. It felt natural—just genuine love and care for others.

The Global Mission Team's mandate falls under the banner of the Great Commission according to Matthew 28:19: "Go and make disciples. "

The vision is to reach lost souls for Christ and promote the Great Commission by positively impacting millions around the world through unconditional love.

The mission of the ministry is to proclaim the Gospel of God to all nations and to empower, equip, and enlighten everyone who comes into the redeeming grace of Jesus Christ through worship, discipleship, intercession, and impartation.

Chapter 4

Belize Answer the Call for Ministry....Boot on the Ground Impartation

The Global Ministry works with orphanages and organizations in other countries that need the Church's help. Aid is also provided to communities affected by disasters and to those facing social or personal hardships.

For example, just last week in the United States, Life Beyond Water and the Church distributed water and dry goods as hurricane relief support to areas in middle Georgia and North Carolina.

The Global Ministry also has guidelines and traditions that help keep us connected and informed. We meet once a month to share ideas and receive ministry updates.

In addition, we plan special recognition services for countries celebrating their independence during that month, usually on the third Sunday.

On Flag Day, we celebrate Haiti.

Chapter 5

Mission Trip to Belize

Belize answered the call for Ministry...Boots on the ground impartation. Overall, I still remember having a wonderful time in Belize going to organizations for girls and babies who had no family support.

These young ladies were so courageous to hear them tell their stories you could see the hand of God working in their lives. We went to and witnessed the ladies giving their lives to God – it was amazing. We also attended the youth fellowship, to hear them worship, sing and praise God, wholeheartedly.

In Punta Gorda, we went to a retirement home to care for a package for seniors. I was amazed to see monkeys overhead in the trees while I was planting cocoa for the love of God. The men on the mission team built indoor bathrooms and kitchens for another mission sister and her husband.

As a member of the mission team, we were required to rise early for morning prayer and devotion. Daily assignments were given so we would be deployed to different organizations partnered with our church.

We did not have contact with the men during the workday. They had their own assignments—building houses, bathrooms, and kitchens—and we would see them at breakfast and sometimes at lunch or dinner.

As missionary women, we were also required to wear long skirts when attending church services. I have experienced religious ceremonies, ordinations, baptisms, and communion, but this experience truly stood out. Since I am not sharing this of my own will alone, but under what I believe is the guidance of the Holy Spirit, I will pause to share this verse:

Psalm 25:5 "Guide me in your truth and teach me for you are God my Savior, and my hope is in you all day long."

You know the story of Jesus washing his disciple's feet in the Bible. Well, I was astonished.

One morning our mission director prayed as she always did, but this morning was different. She and her assistant minister used a bottle of blessed oil and anointed our feet and hands. It was one of the most incredible acts of teaching and serving I had ever experienced in my life.

John 13: 15-16 says, "I have set you an example that you should do as I have done for you. Very truly I tell you, no servant is greater than his master, nor is a messenger greater than the one who sent him."

In that moment, I could see other missionaries begin to cry, and many were deeply moved in what we understood as the presence of the Holy Spirit. It felt like a glimpse of what the Day of Pentecost may have been like in the Upper Room.

I am forever grateful to be part of Team Jesus.

I could go on to say that, out on the mission field, I have seen the power of God move through prayer. One time, the team prayed for our assigned van driver, who told our mission director that he needed healing and deliverance.

To be honest, I cannot fully explain what happened that day in the van, but I can say that when the driver requested prayer, he was overcome, and we believed we witnessed Jehovah Rapha—the Lord who heals—at work. It felt as though a heavy burden was lifted, and peace replaced it.

Acts 32:5 "And we are witnesses to these things, and so is the Holy Spirit, whom God has given to those who obey him."

We also visited a young missionary who had come to the United States to study at Mission University, with plans to return home to serve and make an impact. When his aunt shared that he was ill, and with his mother's permission, the senior team leaders prayed with the family for God's peace, provision, and healing.

The team took photos with him, and we left a love offering.

Later, I learned that I was not allowed to pray for him because I was not a licensed minister in that church. When we left the United States, I was never clearly informed of those rules.

I was wearing a cross necklace at the time, and I was asked where I got it, whether I knew what it represented, and was instructed to remove it and not wear it again. I wrapped it up and brought it home.

Colossians 3:13 says, "Bear with each other and forgive one another if any of you has a grievance against someone. Forgive as the Lord forgave you."

I received that cross for my son's father who has now passed away from pancreatic cancer – such a devastating disease. When I returned home, I asked about it and told him what happened. He said he found it in the warehouse at his job, along with another coworker.

So, at the end of the day, if the real owner needs it, I will be more than happy to give it to them. I could not stay angry with him either, because that brother took care of me – lavished me with baguettes, diamonds, and gold ever since I met him. That's not worth my peace of mind and my mental health. So, I choose forgiveness.

Since this book has taken so many years to come together, I want to share something meaningful: on November 9, 2025, my youngest son, Josh—whom I am well pleased with—was baptized. I also gave him the chain with the cross his father had found and given me.

If his father were still alive, I believe he would have been happy with that decision, especially since he himself was baptized at Solid Rock Church on my birthday.

I remember that song Dre sang about a girl who led him from Judaism to Christianity. In my own life, this man—my husband at the time—was led into faith by this Christian woman. Love is a divine driving force that only God can explain.

When I speak of being blessed, I not only talk about material things, even though those things are nice Lord knows at the end day it is all about Father God and it does matter to him what I am wearing, how my hair is done, if I wrap up with a hair bandana or tie head. Just now this heart focuses and is centered on God. According to Scripture: "You are the salt of the earth, but if salt has lost its taste, how shall its saltiness be restored? It is no longer good for anything except to be thrown out and trampled under people's feet."

Thus, I continue to pursue the mark of a higher calling in Christ Jesus.

I do not clear up rumors. You do not walk out of Ohio Christian University with a Master of Business Administration without doing the work—covering subjects like Walmart, Coca-Cola, Levi Strauss operations and management, ethics, legal contracts, daily devotion assessments, and Dr. John C. Maxwell's 21 Irrefutable Laws of Leadership. My favorite law is the Law of Connection: "Leaders touch a heart before they ask for a hand."

I will make this point: never in my wildest dreams could I ever imagine being a **black Missionary woman on the Mission Field.** However, after watching a video of Dr. John C Maxwell's eye-opening speech, something has shifted in me. He said, "Jesus was the greatest transformational leader that ever lived and yet, He only taught for three years." Roman 12:1 reminds us that our lives should be a living sacrifice, and it captured my attention in a new way. I understood that our purpose more clearly – that every waking and sleeping moment should be an offering to God. I believe that everyone who has breath should praise the Lord and in everything we should give thanks.

After volunteering at my church and serving in the mission room during the week while attending school— helping the mission team prepare for numerous trips – one day, a wonderful mission sister from New York said to me, "You go." She went the extra mile and paid for my mission trip to Haiti, although my first trip was actually to Belize.

Matthew 28:19 says, "Go therefore and make disciples of all nations, baptizing them in the name of the Father, the Son, and the Holy Spirit. "

I was already certified and trained for short-term mission trips by none other than the icon herself, the Doctor. I was no stranger to the team. We attended Sunday worship together, and they were genuinely kind and welcoming.

I can say this honestly because I also worked the mission table every Mission Sunday, collecting donations for mission trips. I will forever be grateful to her and to the members who helped fund my passage on that mission trip.

At the time, my passport had expired, and a Jamaican mission brother offered to pay for it. The mission assistant director provided me with a letter and an itinerary, along with a paid ticket, to take to the Atlanta Passport Office within three days. Within a short time, my new passport arrived by expedited delivery.

Chapter 6

Mission Trip to Haiti Mission of Hope...

My Next trip was the month I was going to Haiti, and I was overly excited.

Here I thought that all the skills that I learned in College would be used to serve the country and the mission field especially because the doctor was opening a transformation school for boys and girls who had proven themselves as tomorrows leaders. Based on my research about transformation leadership, I felt confident – we had this, as they say.

Two of our mission sisters volunteered to serve as interpreters on the trip to Haiti. Their grandparents had taught them to speak Haitian Creole. I was surprised, and honestly moved, to see one of my mission sisters crying while we were volunteering. To make a long story short, the experience was deeply heartfelt.

As I mentioned earlier, I believe there is a need for more Black missionaries serving abroad for many important reasons. Transformational leadership strengths were clearly on display. The power of a transformational

leader is the ability to influence more than one person.
They have the capacity to inspire change within an entire
organization. A true transformational leader
can operate effectively in both secular and Christian
environments.

So here I go again with the blessings of church
family and members.

The mission team and I landed in Port-au-Prince,
Haiti, carrying many suitcases with personal care
products, clothing, shoes medical supplies and medication.
The Doctor surprised us and met us at the airport having
flown in from the States on a connecting flight.

We went to an orphanage for children. The
children were amazing, and our mission team led different
activities such as singing and word games. We also visited a
new school where the teenagers were having orientation.

At one point, the children at the school called us
"white people."

Yes, it was because we were Christian missionaries.
One of my mission sisters explained to them that we were
African American and Christian. Even so, it was difficult
for them to believe, even while looking directly at us.

Nevertheless, by the grace of God, we stood
confidently in the most respectful and humble posture as
servants of God, declaring to the world that we were
African Americans, Christians, and missionaries from our
church in the United States.

As the day continued, we united in prayer and blessed the harvest that God had prepared for us through teaching, gifts, and intercession. We sang and celebrated with the mothers who had completed their training programs.

In the evening, we prepared supplies for our next site. We traveled by van with our Haitian mission guide, who also accompanied us to the market.

Yes, it was serious—we had armed security guards stationed where we slept at night for protection. We were also stopped at checkpoints, and our driver would present identification before we could proceed.

Thank God for my mission director, because whenever we faced difficulty, she would call on one of us to begin praying aloud in the bus. We were trained to pray at a moment's notice. Most times, she would also call on us to sing worship songs while passing through difficult or unsafe areas. We even traveled down to a river and were surprised to see how close people lived to the water, yet how much help was still needed.

We had a challenging time getting back to the airport because of multiple detours during Flag Day. The city was full of celebration—you could see flags everywhere, and it felt like a coordinated national parade. Even the airline gave us Haitian flags in honor of the day.

The food prepared for us was also excellent, prepared by the staff at Aioli. I mention this because it was a refreshing change from our usual meals of sardines, tuna, crackers, and peanuts.

Our missionary men helped build the transformational school with their own hands, brick by brick, for the children.

But honestly, one of the most beautiful moments I witnessed was seeing a donated water well-functioning in the schoolyard. I watched the children run to it and drink clean water—yes, clean water. That memory will forever be in my mind. The kindness of mankind flows like water.

It's still true: where God guides, He provides. Nevertheless, "Therefore, I write these things being absent, lest being present I should use sharpness, according to the power which the Lord hath given me to edification, and not to destruction." (2 Corinthians 13:10).

I asked one of my mission sisters what she would tell the world about Haiti. She said that other countries are blessed to have clean water daily, but it was painful to see the lack of clean water for poorer communities. She wanted people in the States and around the world to understand the value of water.

When I asked why, she reminded me of our visit down by the river. I said yes. While in Haiti, we saw people down by the river using the same water to bathe and wash their clothes. It had garbage, dead animals, and filth flowing through it. When I say that scene hurt me to my core, I mean I was deeply upset that someone filmed it. Once upon a time, decades ago in another country—without the tragedy of a natural disaster like Haiti experienced—I was a young girl bathing and washing my clothes on the side of a river, not because I was poor, but because it was a cultural custom in Jamaica. Yes, Jamaica, Clarendon, at the Chateau River. Those are fond childhood memories I shared with my mom, brothers, and friends. Today, those memories are still priceless. I have not returned to Haiti as a missionary since, nor have I gone personally, because of the United States National Travel Advisory. However, Haiti will remain in my heart and my prayers. I remember the mayor in Haiti telling us when we met him that we were welcome to return and open a hospital that had been newly built. He said all we would need were equipment and supplies.

Haiti, until we meet again—because all my love ever taught me was "Je t'aime, Mon chéri."

Chapter 7

Mission Trip to the Dominican Republic

This time we went to the Dominican Republic. So, as usual, the Global Mission did our due diligence. As stated in our mission mandate, we reach lost souls for Jesus Christ so that all men may be saved by any means necessary.

Therefore, we held our mission meeting and addressed the agenda. The customary practice is to begin with an opening prayer and welcoming our guests.

As part of the team, I was not a minister, so I served in every area as needed.

We also completed a distribution overview, which addressed what would be needed for the population we would serve. We always packed personal care products, including toothpaste, soap, toothbrushes, washcloths, lotion, and shampoo. We also included clothing for children, separating boys' items from girls' items, as well as clothing and shoes for women and men. We brought linens and school supplies. If they needed it, it was in the suitcases.

We completed a cultural awareness refresher course, including brushing up on basic Spanish. Yes, we had Spanish classes before going to Belize, and we also had French and Creole training before Haiti. However, as we did more missions, we discovered that English is truly a universal language.

I must note that during the month of each trip, an announcement was made during Sunday service for new team members to join the mission team, along with a request for financial support. This meant each participant often had to pay their own way, so having a sponsor was important.

My first two trips were covered by a sponsor, but I paid my own way for the Dominican Republic and my second trip to Belize. I heard we had a mission budget, but I never saw it. I also heard that the pastor would cover the cost of going to Africa; however, that never happened.

As a result, I did not have the funds to go with the mission team to Africa. I am not saying this as a negative reflection on anyone. I say this simply because trips to Africa are very costly and can now run up to $4,000 per person.

However, if the church had sent me, I would have gone.

When the day came, as usual, we all met at our church. The pastor prayed with us first, and then the charter van picked us up and took us to the airport. They also picked us up when we returned from our mission trip. It was an exceptionally good company, and they provided excellent customer service.

On this mission trip, we went to a basic school where we sang and praised God with the children. They all looked so lovely in their school uniforms, and they sang for us, "This Is the Day." It was a beautiful moment. The mission team helped the mothers prepare lunch for the children, as the pastor had requested.

We also visited another wonderful school where we spent almost the entire day. The group included children from babies to teenagers. The young girls were exceptionally talented ballet dancers.

At the orphanage, the owners—a husband-and-wife team who were also, the administrators—gave us a full tour. The property was well-kept and beautiful. The teachers at the school were truly kind and professional.

We also had an amazing church service led by none other than our mission director.

What made this especially meaningful was that this church was sponsored by our pastor, and our missionary men built a beautiful sanctuary with their own hands. It was a sacred gift of love to God's people. I did not remember to report this to the pastor and our congregation, but the people showed in their actions how much they love this church.

This was a special mission trip because we were invited to Pastor R's home for his birthday. His wife and children were wonderful hosts, and they cooked for us a feast fit for a king. The meal was large and delicious.

My favorite part was the blend of different fruits used to make juice and the mashed cassava they called yuca. It was a wonderful celebration, and we left a gift from our church—or perhaps I should say from our pastors in the States.

Chapter 8

A Mission for Men's Rehabilitation

We went to a men's rehabilitation home and held services there. This was the first time I had seen our missionary men involved in outreach and anointed prayer services, because they were usually building bathrooms, kitchens, schools, and churches on these trips.

The men at the rehabilitation home also shared their testimonies about how Jesus Christ had saved their lives.

They also testified about what a blessing the rehabilitation center was, because it kept them off the street and provided them with a place to live and food to eat. This part of the ministry was new to me from my earlier trips and was very eye-opening.

The deacons prayed with the men, and we sowed an offering of faith and continued strength, then we left. We also visited a retirement home and spent quality time with the elderly. You could see on their faces that they enjoyed our visit. At the end of the visit, the staff thanked us for coming to worship with them. The retirement home was clean, and most importantly, the residents looked well cared for and happy.

I spoke with a staff member who told me she was from Haiti, which surprised me because we were in the

Dominican Republic. She was kind and very caring toward her patients.

Nevertheless, as God would have it, the next day we lined up with patients to enter the hospital and volunteer in the clinic, helping the medical staff provide needed care. My team of three ended up serving as assistants to the orthopedic doctor.

We helped provide treatment to patients who needed immediate care, as directed by the doctor, and others who were being assessed for orthopedic surgery by the Dr. Almanzar Foundation and Orlando Martinez Fundación medical team.

It was an unbelievably valuable experience to see the medical team paying it forward. It was especially impressive considering the language barriers, while other staff were assigned to different units.

I must admit, we had some time between our vocational assignments, and the mission director asked the driver to take us by the river. I enjoyed it, since I had not been to a river in years.

Our trip was successful, and on that day, we distributed all the supplies we had brought for the children and the community.

The surprise came when we returned to the church and our pastor and his team had flowers and balloons waiting for us.

I was shocked, but it was very nice.

I learned that all things work together for those who love the Lord. Subsequently, when you are part of the Global Mission Ministry, you embrace all nations, and in return, they embrace you. I can say with every step that God has kept me.

Respectfully, I thank God for all the members who have supported me and the team, and for following the four pillars of mission: giving, praying, sending, and allowing me to follow the mandate of going.

I give thanks. According to the word of the Lord, "In everything give thanks."

Therefore, I also give thanks to everyone who has stood with me and at times, cared for me.
May we continue to honor God with the gifts He has given us all. The work reaps a great harvest of souls for Jesus Christ, so let us not become weary in doing good.

Chapter 9

The Second Mission Trip to Belize

Mission Work: Look At Rapha 2024

It has been six months since I stopped using the cane after a bad fall. I survived a heart attack and had heart surgery. I lost my sons' father, my ex-husband, my former mother-in-law, my children's grandmother, my dad, my mom, and my two younger brothers—one of whom was my best friend. Lord, I am still here by the grace of God. The Lord absolutely loves me.

Last month, I took my second trip back to Belize in Central America. The massive number of miracles my eyes beheld—may God be glorified.

Season of Miracles

As of May 2024, they are building tiny homes in Belize, just like in Africa. Our team was fortunate to help paint the homes that the Global Mission Ministry men had built. We even received help from the students at Living Word Christian School of Ministry.

The missionary house was double in size, and they were still working on it while I was there—glory to God.

Also, while I was there, Jesus did it again. I was praying with a lady in a church in Toledo. I barely laid my hands in hers, and she was filled with the Holy Spirit and passed out. I honestly did not know what to do except catch her and help her to the floor. I called out to a sister from the Living Word Christian Ministry for help, and she assisted me.
That's how amazing my God is!

If I had to name this mission trip the way my old director used to—like "Boot on the Ground" or "Mission Impartation" —I would call it a "Mission of Miracles."
I myself was being healed right there on the mission field. This was a healing experience in the Mayan village, and not just for me.

Once, I ministered to a man who had spent seventeen years in prison. He said he was innocent of the crime. However, he also said he was guilty of other terrible things, just not what they said he had done.

He told me that he did not believe in God, but I asked him to consider that the fact he was in that church, on that day, was a miracle.

I told him it was God's love for him, because I had gotten up from my sick bed and traveled halfway around the world to ask him if he would accept Jesus Christ as his Lord and Savior—and he said yes. Oh, my Lord.

Thus, with the help of a senior minister, a wonderful woman of God, she pulled out her phone, opened the prayer of salvation, and handed me the phone so I could lead him in that special prayer of salvation. Matthew 28:19 says, "Go therefore and make disciples of all nations, baptizing them in the name of the Father, the Son, and the Holy Spirit."

Heaven rejoiced.

Mark 16:16 says, "He who believes and is baptized will be saved, but he who does not believe will be condemned. And these signs will follow those who believe: In My name they will cast out demons; they will speak with new tongues."

Miraculously, I also witnessed a newborn baby being blessed in the jungle of the Mayan village, with the help of a dear minister, Sunshine.

I had the opportunity to pray for a man who became ill and needed prayer to make it home safely to his family in Georgia. The Lord Jehovah Rapha stood up for him that day. Yes, I mean that—the weapon may form, but it will never prosper, declares the Lord. But this is his story to tell. I also had the opportunity to help a sister write her business plan for an Aid to Trade business meeting. I had firsthand exposure to Punta Gorda's resources and visited both Mayan and Garifuna villages in Belize.

My main intention is to bring positive light for the edification of God's people. May they forever be blessed and have no lack.

Chapter 10

My Consistent Volunteer Services

Barbara Walters once said, "What is the point of doing something if you're not going to tell someone about it?" The Georgia Mass Choir also sang, "Tell it." Well, if you knew me before the pandemic, you would know I volunteered and served at my church to help my pastor build and grow his ministry. He took flights like they were car rides. That is not a rumor—he would fly in for Sunday worship to avoid traffic because we have three separate locations.

As you already know, since 2016, I have volunteered with the Global Mission Ministry and have served around the world. I have participated in every march for justice with my church, including Black Lives Matter events and prayer walks—more than once. I show up for every Dr. Martin Luther King Jr. parade, work in the community, and help feed the homeless at Gateway in Atlanta, including women and children.

I also volunteer with the Caribbean Association of Georgia and have worked with other board members, serving briefly as the first female Sergeant-at-Arms. I also enjoy volunteering with Mama Christmas in McDonough. When my son was young, I volunteered at his elementary school 50 and served on the Parent-Teacher Association

(PTA) at Walnut Creek Elementary School. I also took students on school trips to the State Capitol and met some very interesting people. I ride my bike, play basketball — yes, kick a football —and I praise and dance my socks off.

I am one of the first women in Henry County to have opened my home for a campaign event supporting the former two-term President Barack Obama, working with grassroots organizations and Young Democrats, canvassing for my local representative and mayor. That represents over two decades of giving back. I did not list these things for an award. If the truth be told, there is much more I cannot even list.

I pray that God gives my community the strength to continue, because I know my community matters. The Bible says we should not become weary in doing good. I still recall days when Bruce, the first Black commissioner of Henry County, ran and held his position, or when Val Samuel, a community organizer, and he ran for his seat in Henry County. All of this was nearly two decades ago. Today, we have Sandra Vincent as the Mayor of McDonough, Georgia—a genuinely kind woman.

Thanks to the gentleman who taught me the art of canvassing for his campaign. This led me to make an impact in my career as a field Census representative Supervisor, putting Hampton, Georgia, on the map. I intend to stay focused and move forward. I am simply stating the level of my civic involvement before COVID-19.

I believe the government should look at all statistics, not just large datasets on who contracted the virus, but also the side effects from 51 vaccinations. Everyone knows microdata does not always capture the full picture.

Ever since I went to the emergency room on March 20th, at the height of the COVID-19 pandemic, my life has not been the same. I am not an old woman by any means, but there are days when I cannot get out of bed. My daughter and my sons have had to care for me since the pandemic. It has been over three years, with more than thirty doctor's visits, and two rounds of physical therapy to learn how to walk without a cane after a fall. Yet Social Security still does not provide or pay any of my benefits.

I do not know if others have experienced side effects like mine—weakness in the muscles and legs, feeling like they have a mind of their own. I have more side effects, but they are personal. As the saying goes, "The room is too small for all of us, " and this is between my doctor and me. And I can still laugh, because laughter is good medicine. Please feel free to use this information, because each experience teaches another. I have been to physical therapy twice.

Yes, I had a fall, but I told the security guards in the parking lot, who helped me up and took me to my truck, that I would be fine. One of them walked me to my truck but did not report the incident to the police officer. I also want to thank my brother, who brought me lemonade when I fell. I wish I knew his name so I could personally say thank you. 52 As of today, I have been to physical therapy twice to learn how to walk on my own and to use a cane for balance, so I do not fall again. Now, I can walk short distances. I am working in decency and order according to God's will.

Since I am a praying woman, I know God has me, and He has answered every prayer—not because of what I do, but because of who He is. I have learned to use Google Docs, typing with one finger at a time. My prayers are atomic. Every time I pray, I believe the heavens are opened, and my prayers reach God. I am more empowered today than I was yesterday.

In conclusion, when you complete a School of Ministry to be a Minister with a 96.5 overall grade and lose six close family members in less than two years, it wakes you up. I no longer have the tolerance for with fake behavior in people, the goal is all about integrity and edifying God people even on Mondays.

Missionary Prayer

LORD JESUS, I thank you for giving us the heart of grace and empathy of awareness to provide good services to all mankind and those in need emotionally, spiritually, physically, and financially. Thank you for giving us the courage and strength to continue the Lord's work with a kind and caring heart.

Father, we ask that through the Holy Spirit, You will guide us to be fair and honest when dealing with all your people regardless of gender, race, religion, creed, or nationality. Lord give us eyes to see, ears to hear wisdom to operate in decency and order.

May we have spiritual gifts to bring souls to You. May we have healing hands, like angels to care for Your people. May we have strong feet, like Moses, to go the distance to ensure a great harvest to edify Your name.

May we have more than enough oil in our lamps to shine through the darkness. May we have enough bread and water to feed Your people. May we all have divine protection and favor in Jesus' name.

May we be good stewards of each other starting at home in our churches, school communities, states, countries and nation. May We always be on our best behavior and uphold the integrity of God and Country.

Father, accordingly, we accept your will as you stated
Matthew 28:18-20: "And Jesus came and said to them, 'All authority in heaven and on earth has been given to me. Go therefore and make disciples of all nations, baptizing them in the name of the Father and of the Son and of the Holy Spirit, teaching them to observe all that I have commanded you. And behold, I am with you always, to the end of the age.'"

In Jesus name we pray, thank You. And God's people say, Amen and Amen.

Missionary Julian Marie Walker

1. Have you ever heard of Jesus Christ and what they did to him? (Isaiah 53:5, "But he was pierced for our transgressions. He was crushed for our iniquities; upon him was the chastisement that brought us peace, and with his wounds, we are healed.")

2. Do you believe in him? (John 3:16, "For God so loved the world, that he gave his only Son, that whoever believes in him should not perish but have eternal life.")

3. If you die today, will you go to heaven? (Roman 6:23, "For the wages of sin is death, but the gift of God is eternal life in Christ Jesus our Lord.")

4.If you are not sure. Would you accept Jesus as your Lord and Savior? (John 14:6, "Jesus said to him, 'I am the way, and the truth, and the life. No one comes to the father except through me.)

Please read this prayer of Salvation. If you agree, sign your name as the confession of your faith.

Prayer for Salvation Agreement

Heavenly Father, my sincere apology for taking so long to come to you. I am here now asking forgiveness for all my past sins.

Lord, I want you to cleanse me and give me a clean heart to serve you. I repent of my worldly ways and believe that you die on the cross and rise on the third day for me. I vow to worship and serve you for the rest of my life. In the name of the Father, Jesus Christ his Son, and the Holy Spirit.

I pray, Amen.

Sign your name_____________________________________

As a confession of your faith, this day you have been saved by grace according to the word of God that Jesus is your Lord and Savior without any coercion or force from anyone. In Jesus's mighty name. You are now saved. Amen

Missionary Julian Marie Walker

Holy Ghost on Fire: A Missionary Bible Talk

1. It is good to seek out a Bible-based church to praise God.
2. It is recommended you take the second part of your faith more intentionally by getting baptized in your local church.

There are three reasons why:

John 3:5 says, "Jesus answered, 'Truly, truly, I say to you, unless one is born of water and the Spirit, he cannot enter the kingdom of God.'"

Mark 16:16 states,
"Whoever believes and is baptized will be saved, but whoever does not believe will be condemned."

Matthew 28:19, "Go therefore and make disciples of all nations, baptizing them in the name of the Father and of the Son and the Holy Spirit." God loves your praise and obedience, and I will keep you in my prayers always.

Sincerely, Missionary Julian M. Walker

Workbook Discussion

1. What you should know before taking this next step, and the meaning of getting baptized.

Matthew 3:13-17 Then Jesus came from Galilee to Jordan to be baptized by John. 14 But John tried to deter him, saying, "I need to be baptized by you, and do you come to me?" 15 Jesus replied, "Let it be so now; it is proper for us to do this to fulfill all righteousness." Then John consented. 16 As soon as
Jesus was baptized; he went up out of the water. At that moment, heaven was opened, and he saw the Spirit of God descending like a dove and alighting on him. 17 And a voice from heaven said, "This is my Son, whom I love; with him I am well pleased."

2. The scripture shows that Jesus was also baptized, are you willing to be baptized?
Scripture reads as: 17 Therefore if any man be in Christ, he is a new creature: old things are passed away; behold, all things are become new. 2 Corinthians 5:17

3. Why? It is an expression of your faith Journey. Scripture states Ephesians 2:8-9 For it is by grace you have been saved, through faith—and this is not from yourselves, it is the gift of God— 9 not by works, so that no one can boast.

4. When you get baptized, there is no sprinkle of water on your head that is called a baby declaration. Getting baptized is going in water and coming out filled with the Holy Spirit.

God bless you. My prayer is that you are intentional about your transformation by getting baptized in your local Bible-based Church.

About the Author

Ms. Julian Marie Walker was born in Clarendon, Jamaica, West Indies. She lived in New York for over thirty years and attended the Metropolitan College of New York, where she earned a bachelor's degree in Professional Studies. She is also a graduate of Ohio Christian University, where she earned a master's degree in Business Administration.

She has been blessed by God as a mother of five children, five grandchildren, and one great-grandchild.

She attends and is a member of Tabernacle of Praise Church International in Georgia, where she serves as a Deaconess, she is part of the intercessory prayer team and serves on the Global Mission Team. One of her passions is missionary work, both locally and internationally, including service in Belize, Haiti, and the Dominican Republic.

She has worked in food distribution, fellowship outreach, hospitals and medical clinics, and has visited the elderly and orphanages, as well as participated in building schools and churches. Ms. Walker has also volunteered with the Caribbean Association of Georgia as the first-ever female Sergeant-at-Arms.

Ms. Walker is a well-cultured, caring Christian with a godly heritage, committed to faith, moral ethics, and integrity, with a desire to further the growth of this organization through the advancement and empowerment of all people—not only in her community and regardless of nationality, but to all people.

Thus, she has a servant's heart and believes that great servants make the greatest leaders in history. Her volunteering, work experience, and contributions reflect her character and achievements, grounded in her mother's greatest gift to her: the gift of service and prayer.

Acknowledgments

Jesus Christ is Lord!

Dedication

In memories of my mother, Victoria Marie Brown-Hyde and my dad, Justin Walker. Also, my brother, TrooperUpton J. Walker. I am thankful for the strength of God, my children, grandchildren, Camilla, Theisman, Ticori, Tennessee, and Jennifer, and my great-grandson, Kyree. I am also thankful for my nieces and nephews, as well as my former deans, teachers, and professors.

Thank you, Dr. Nelson, for helping me publish my books.

I pray for all missionaries around the world for continued protection and provision.

Notes

65
65

Notes

Notes

Notes

Notes

Notes

70